red rhino
bOOks®
NONFICTION

Area 51	Monsters on Land
Cloning	Seven Wonders of the Ancient World
Drones	**Virtual Reality**
Fault Lines	
Great Spies of the World	Witchcraft
Monsters of the Deep	Wormholes

SADDLEBACK
EDUCATIONAL PUBLISHING
www.sdlback.com

ISBN-13: 978-1-68021-036-1
ISBN-10: 1-68021-036-X
eBook: 978-1-63078-343-3

Printed in Singapore by Craft Print International Ltd
0000/CA00000000

19 18 17 16 15   1 2 3 4 5

TABLE OF CONTENTS

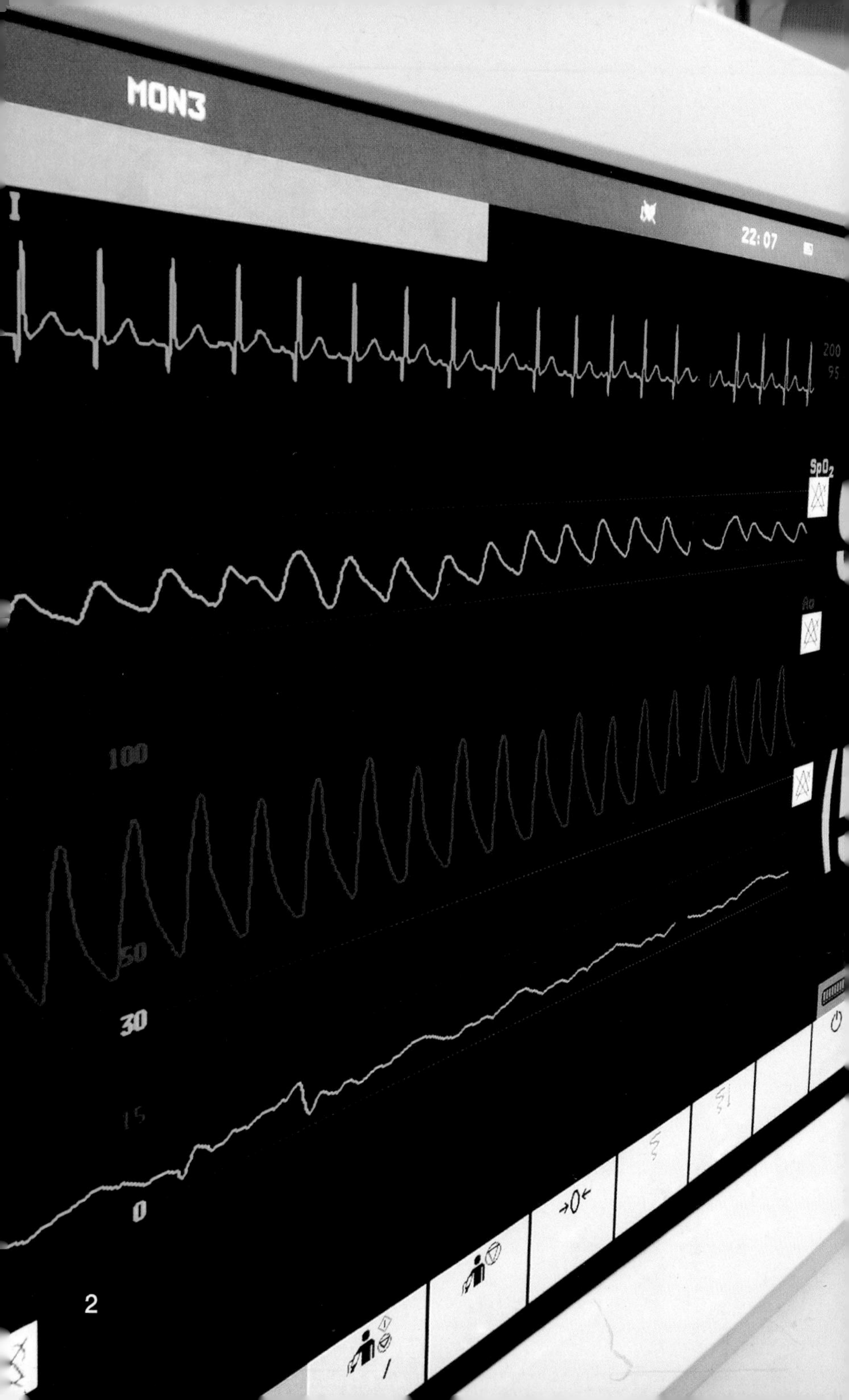
MON3
I
22:07
200
95
SpO2
Ao
100
50
30
15
0

Chapter 1
HAVE A HEART

She's sick.

It is hard to breathe.

She's tired.

All the time.

So she sleeps.

It is hard to walk.

She can't work.

What's wrong?

The doctor has an idea.

She thinks it's the woman's heart.

It's sick.

How can she be sure?

A machine will help.

It is a special *x-ray* machine.

The woman lies on a table.

The machine takes pictures.

Click, click, click.

These are not normal pictures.
They are 3-D pictures.
They show the woman's heart.
The doctor looks.
She still can't tell what's wrong.
No problem.
She turns on a device.
It turns the x-rays into sound.
It squeezes the *sound waves*.
Molds them like clay.

Up pops a human heart.

Floating.

Like a balloon in the air.

This is no toy.

It's a *hologram*.

A 3-D *image* of the woman's heart.

The doctor looks.
She spins the image.
Like a ball.
She turns it up.
Then down.

She sees what's wrong.
It can be fixed.
The woman won't
need *surgery*.
She will soon be well.
Thanks to the virtual heart.

Does this sound like
science fiction?
It's not.
It's one of the uses of
virtual reality.

Chapter 2

THE SOMETIMES REAL WORLD

Virtual reality.

VR for short.

It seems real.

But it is created by computers.

Why does it seem real?

It has three *dimensions*.

Height.

Width.

Depth.

Just like the real world.

You can play in the virtual world.

Work.

Take trips.

Meet new people.

You can try new things.

Fly a jet.

Race a car.

Walk on Mars.

Hold a person's heart in your hand.

It's fun to think about.
VR has been in books.
On TV.
In movies.
Like *Tron*.
It came out in 1982.

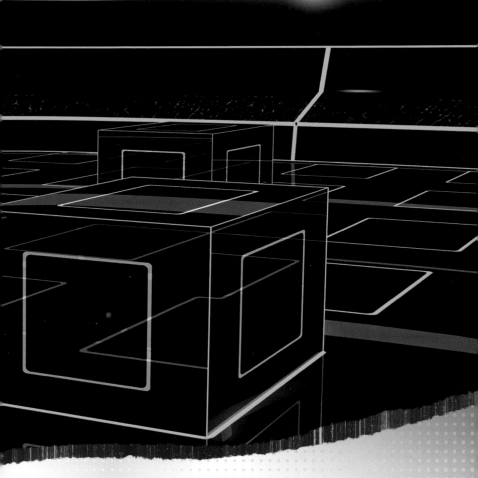

Another came out in 2010.

Tron: Legacy.

It continues the story.

It is all about virtual reality.

A father builds a *digital* world.

But he gets lost inside it.

His son looks for him there.

VR is great for games.

It takes you to different worlds.

You can explore a sunken ship.

Search for gold.

Kill aliens.

Play sports.

GAME ON
Virtual Boy was the first game where players had to wear a mask-like headset.

Chapter 3
VR HISTORY

How did VR get its start?

The first step was in 1833.

Charles Wheatstone built a
set of glasses.

He called it a *stereoscope* viewer.

Inside were two photos.

People looked through the *lens*.

The two images became one.

A 3-D image.

People loved it.

Thirty years went by.

Artists liked 3-D too.

Some had an idea.

They painted on curved screens.

Viewers would stand on a stage.

The painting was around them.

It seemed real.

They were part of the art.

17

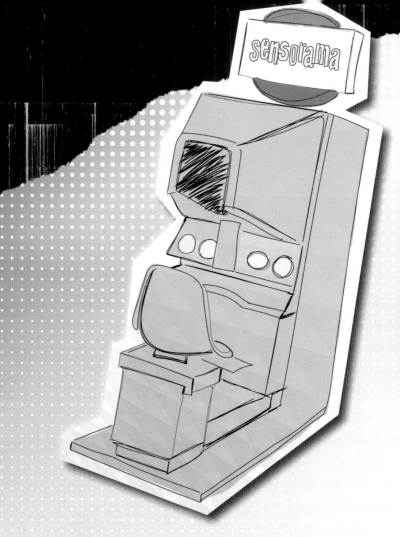

VR took a step forward in 1960.

Morton Heilig loved movies.

He wanted to make them more real.

He built a machine.

Sensorama.

It had a small screen.

It had speakers and fans.

Whoosh!

People could feel the wind.

Sniff!

People could smell the sea.

People loved it.

But the machine broke easily.

People wanted better VR worlds.

They would get them.

How?

With computers.

Chapter 4

COMPUTER CRAZE

The first computers were huge.

They filled a room.

They were slow too.

But they could be programmed.

They could work with tools.

Tools that people wore.

EARLY COMPUTERS

This let computers control
people's senses.
Hearing.
Sight.
Sound.
Movement.
People sensed the images were real.

Ivan Sutherland was one of
the first to do this.
He worked with early
computers.
He made the first VR tool.

It was 1968.
Sutherland built a *headset*.
Part of it hung from the ceiling.
It was heavy.
His students would put it on.
They looked like robots with
thick glasses.

They saw images.

They could turn their heads.

The picture would still be there.

It was all around them.

Like it was real.

This first headset worked.

More were invented.

They got smaller.

Computers got smarter.

VR became more real.

Chapter 5
HELMET HEADS

VR made big leaps in the 1970s.
The Air Force began using VR helmets.
Pilots learned to fly with them.
It was safer.
And cheaper than
having a real
jet crash.

HEAD-MOUNTED DISPLAY

The pilots put on helmets.

Head-mounted displays.

HMDs for short.

To the pilots it seemed real.

They were in a cockpit.

They could look up.

Down.

To the side.

Out the window.

They could see the controls.

Push the buttons.

How does this work?

HMDs have two screens.

One for each eye.

This tricks people's eyes.

They think they are seeing things for real.

But it's all virtual.

VR has taken off since then.

People are testing new tools.

Joysticks.

A *mouse*.

Even gloves.

Chapter 6
IF THE GLOVE FITS

VR helmets work well.

People think they are in another world.

But what about the sense of touch?

That's where wired gloves come in.

They have *sensors*.

The first one came out in the 1980s.

The gloves talk to a computer.

They send messages using *fiber optics*.

These are thin strands of glass.

Bend a finger.

The computer knows.

Make a fist.

The computer knows that too.

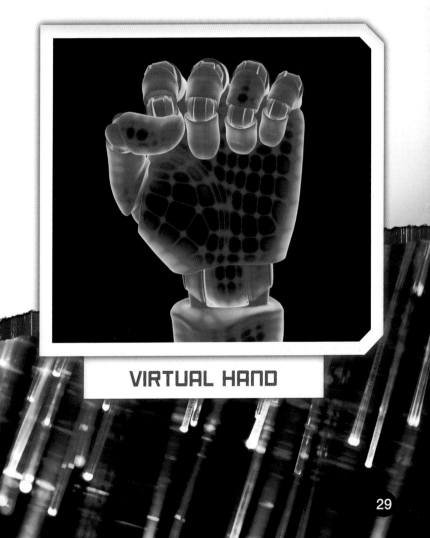

VIRTUAL HAND

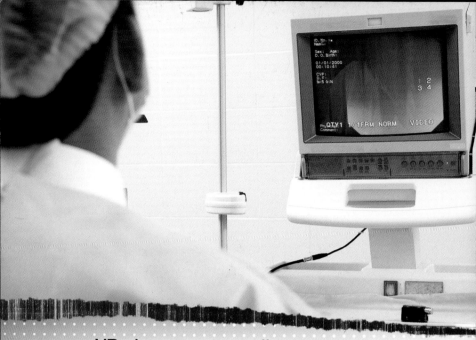

VR gloves can save lives.

How?

Doctors can use them.

It was 1997.

A man was sick.

A doctor had to operate.

The doctor was in Italy.

The man was 1,000 miles away.

The doctor put on a VR glove.

He looked at a video screen.

The glove moved a *robotic* arm.

The doctor operated with VR.

 It was a success!

Today we can see the virtual world.

But we can't feel it.

Hot.

Cold.

Rough.

Smooth.

One day we will.

New gloves are being tested.

They will trick our sense of touch.

THAT'S COOL
Jaron Lanier first used the term "virtual reality" in 1984. His company made the first VR glove people could buy in 1987.

Bodysuits are cool too.
They let you move through a virtual
world.
They look like costumes.
They have wires.
A headset.
Gloves.
The suits have sensors.
They follow a person's moves.
Swing a bat.
Throw a ball.
Run.
The computer knows what
the person is doing.
It can change what the
person sees.
This is where VR gets real.

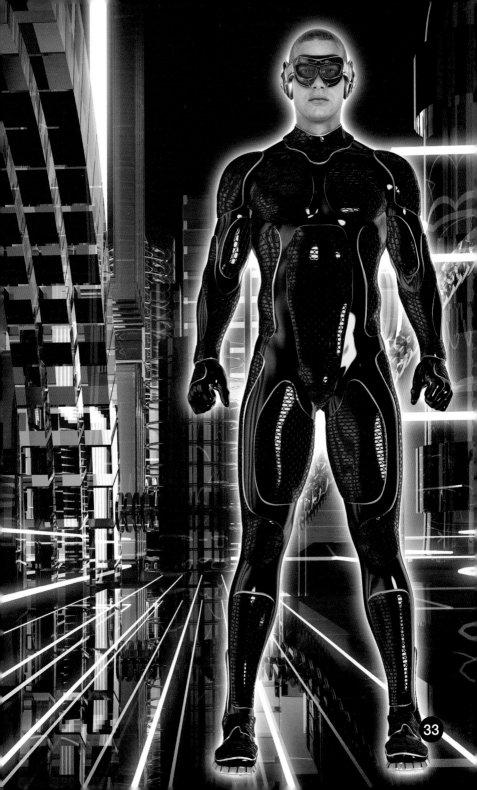

Chapter 7

HOLOGRAMS

Remember the 3-D heart?

It was a hologram.

Holograms are another part of VR.

Holograms blend reality and illusion.

Companies are using this now.

People can put on a headset.

Walk on virtual streets.

Live in virtual houses.

THAT'S COOL
New VR headsets are being developed. Some will hook up to smartphones. VR goes mobile.

It's all a hologram.

But it feels real.

Other people can be there too.

They just have to have a headset.

It's like a big video game.

With millions of people.

Many companies have hologram devices.

Sony makes one.

Put it on.

Shine light on a cartoon robot.

The robot will close its eyes.

Microsoft has a tinted *visor*.

It puts holograms on top of

the real world.

A VR glass on a real table.

A VR monster in your bedroom.

Fantasies become real.

You can use it for work.

Or for fun.

THAT'S COOL
Scientists want to use a
hologram visor to explore
Mars.

37

Chapter 8
VIRTUAL HEALING

VR can help heal people.

Not just those with bad hearts.

Some people can't walk.

Their brains won't let them.

They put on a helmet.

It tells them where to put their feet.

They can walk.

Some for the first time.

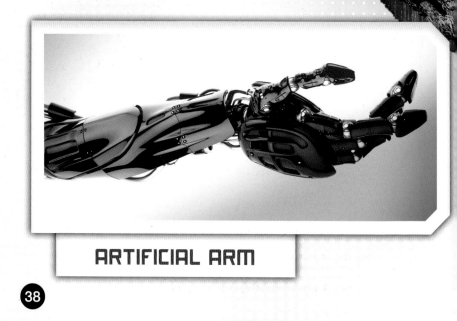

ARTIFICIAL ARM

People lose arms and legs.

Their brains think the limbs are still there.

Toes go numb.

Hands hurt.

The pain is bad.

It's not real.

It's in the person's mind.

VR can make the pain go away.

The person puts on a VR device.

It is wired to a computer.

The person thinks about his missing arm.

He tries to move it.

A virtual arm moves instead.

On a computer.

He plays a racing game.

Zoom!

The pain slowly goes away.

GAME ON

Scientists at the University of Washington have made a VR game. Burn victims can play it. They throw snowballs. Their pain is reduced.

Chapter 9
TAKING A TRIP

Field trips are fun.

You learn new things.

See new places.

Can you go anywhere you want?

Not really.

But one day you might.

You will never leave the classroom.

But it will feel like you did.

It's a virtual field trip.

Travel to the Arctic.

See polar bears and seals.

Go around the world.

Meet different *cultures*.

You will wear goggles.

Like HMDs.

Computers will send images to the goggles.

You will feel like you are traveling.

You might visit a volcano.

Look inside.

Virtual field trips can go anywhere.

Walk on the sea floor.

Travel back in time.

See a dinosaur.

THAT'S COOL

The first virtual field trip came out in 1995. It let students explore the Antarctic.

Chapter 10
THE GOOD AND BAD

New VR tools are made every year.

We are just starting to see what they can do.

VR can help doctors.

Make work easier.

Train people more safely.

But not everyone sees VR as good.

Some think it will become too real.

People won't want to talk.

They'll ignore friends.

They won't leave home.

They'll live in a make-believe world.

VR will take over their lives.

Virtual reality.
It feels real.
It is meant to.
That can be good.
Or bad.
It depends how it is used.

Are you ready to explore new worlds?
Do things no one has done before?
You will.
The virtual world is here.
And it is more real every day.

GLOSSARY

cultures: ways of life

depth: how deep something is

digital: computer information in the form of 0s and 1s

dimensions: the size of something

fiber optics: thin strands of glass that use light to move information

headset: an electronic tool worn around the head; it receives and sends information

hologram: an image with width, height, and length

image: a picture

joystick: a control lever

lens: a piece of curved glass that is focusing on an object

mouse: a device that controls a computer

robotic: relating to robots

sensors: devices that spot and react to light, heat, or movement

sound waves: ripple-like disturbances in the air that carry sound forward

stereoscope: device that creates the fantasy of 3-D images

surgery: a medical treatment that involves cutting a person open

virtual reality: a computer world that simulates a three-dimensional setting

visor: a screen for the eyes

width: thickness

x-ray: high-energy waves that can penetrate a solid object and take pictures

TAKE A LOOK INSIDE

DRONES

Chapter 3

WORKING FOR US

Drones have a lot of uses.
They go where we cannot.

They see inside volcanoes.
Spy for us in war.
Save wild animals.
Find lost hikers.
Track wildfires.
Watch storms.
Dive into the ocean.

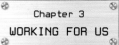

14

15

Chapter 5
SEARCH AND RESCUE

Drones save people too.
They can be used to search.
They can see in rain and snow.
They can see in the dark.
This helps them find lost hikers.

How does a drone search?
It flies over hiking paths.
It films the land.
It can see body heat.
This is how it finds people.

Rescue workers look at the films.
They know where to search.
Lost people are found.

DRONE DATA

Many people own drones. Some want to use their drones to help find lost people. They offer to help local search and rescue teams.

Some roads are still blocked today.
But drones don't need roads.
They need airspace.
They need a place to land.

Experts tested drones in Haiti.
The tests worked.
Drones got to the towns.
They brought medicine.
Sick people got help.

MAP OF HAITI

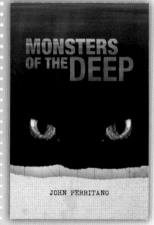

red rhino books® NONFICTION

DRONES
SUSAN HENNEBERG
9781680210293

MONSTERS OF THE DEEP
JOHN PERRITANO
9781680210286

JOHN PERRITANO
MONSTERS on Land
9781680210309

WORMHOLES
JOHN PERRITANO
9781680210330

VIRTUAL REALITY
JOHN PERRITANO
9781680210361

Witchcraft
CAROL PIZER
9781680210323

AREA 51
9781680210316

FAULT LINES
JOHN PERRITANO
9781680210538

CLONING
SUSAN HENNEBERG
9781680210347

SEVEN WONDERS of the ANCIENT WORLD
ARIANNE McHUGH
9781680210354